D0402799

WORDS OF LOVE

WORDS OF LOVE

Edited by Leah S. Matthews

A THOMAS DUNNE BOOK

St. Martin's Press
New York

Library of Congress Cataloging-in-Publication Data

Matthews, Leah S.
    Words of love / Leah S. Matthews.
        p.   cm.
    "A Thomas Dunne book."
    ISBN 0-312-07235-X
    1. Love—Literary collections.   I. Title.
  PN6071.L7M38   1992
  808.8'0354—dc20   91-37717
                                                         CIP

First published in Great Britain by Judy Piatkus (Publishers) Limited. First published in the United States by Salem House, a member of Merrimack Publishers' Circle.

Second U.S. Edition: February 1992
10 9 8 7 6 5 4 3 2

CONTENTS

MEETING♥ ♥ ♥

. . . All the mystery of her beauty is in the brilliance, the enigma of her eyes. I have never seen such a beautiful woman. But I did not ask for an introduction . . . I think talking to her might disturb and embarrass me.

Marcel Proust (1871–1922) talking about Comtesse Greffulhe
in a letter to Montesquiou

A lady's imagination is very rapid; it jumps from admiration to love, from love to matrimony, in a moment.

Jane Austen
Pride and Prejudice, 1813

Sudden love takes the longest time to be cured.

La Bruyère
Of the Affections, Characters 1688

WILLIAM SHAKESPEARE
AS YOU LIKE IT

Rosalind: . . . for your brother and my sister no sooner met but they looked; no sooner looked but they loved; no sooner loved but they sighed; no sooner sighed but they asked one another the reason; no sooner knew the reason but they sought the remedy: and in these degrees have they made a pair of stairs to marriage, which they will climb incontinent, or else be incontinent before marriage: they are in the very wrath of love, and they will together; clubs cannot part them.

Act V: Scene 2

LEO TOLSTOY
ANNA KARENINA

At four o'clock that afternoon Levin stepped out of a hired sleigh at the Zoological Gardens and, with beating heart, turned along the path to the ice-hills and the skating-ground, sure of finding Kitty there, as he had seen the Shcherbatsky's carriage at the entrance . . .

. . . He knew she was there by the joy and the terror that seized his heart. She was standing talking to a lady at the opposite end of the rink. There was apparently nothing particularly striking either in her dress or her attitude; but for Levin it was as easy to find her in that crowd as to see a rose among nettles. She made everything bright. She was the smile that shed light on all around her. 'Can I really step on to the ice and go up to her?' he wondered. The spot where she stood seemed to him unapproachable holy ground and there was one moment when he nearly turned away, so filled with awe was he. He had to make an effort and reason with himself that all sorts of people were moving about her and that he too might come there just to skate. He walked down, for a long while averting his eyes from her, as though she were the sun, but seeing her, as one sees the sun, without looking.

FRANÇOISE SAGAN
BONJOUR TRISTESSE

He was not at all ridiculous. I thought he was kind, already half in love with me, and that it would be nice to be in love with him too. I put my arms round his neck and my cheek against his. He had broad shoulders and his body felt hard against mine.

'You're very sweet, Cyril,' I murmured. 'You shall be a brother to me.'

He folded his arms round me with an angry little exclamation, and gently pulled me out of the boat. He held me close against him, my head on his shoulder. At that moment I loved him. In the morning light he was as golden, as soft, as gentle as myself. He was protecting me. As his lips touched mine we both began to tremble, and the pleasure of our kiss was untinged by shame or regret, merely a deep searching interrupted every now and then by whispers. I broke away and swam towards the boat, which was drifting out. I dipped my face into the water to refresh it. The water was green. A feeling of reckless happiness came over me.

♥

ANNE FRANK'S DIARY

Sunday morning, just before eleven o'clock
16th April, 1944

Darlingest Kitty,

Remember yesterday's date, for it is a very important day in my life. Surely it is a great day for every girl when she receives her first kiss? Well, then, it is just as important for me too! Bram's kiss on my right cheek doesn't count any more, likewise the one from Mr. Walker on my right hand.

How did I suddenly come by this kiss? Well, I will tell you.

Yesterday evening at eight o'clock I was sitting with Peter on his divan. It wasn't long before his arm went round me. 'Let's move up a bit,' I said, 'then I don't bump my head against the cupboard.' He moved up, almost into the corner, I laid my arm under his and across his back, and he just about buried me, because his arm was hanging on my shoulder.

Now we've sat like this on other occasions, but never so close together as yesterday. He held me firmly against him, my left shoulder against his chest; already my heart began to beat faster, but we had not finished yet. He didn't rest until my head was on his shoulder and his against it. When I sat upright again after about five minutes, he soon took my head in his hands and laid it against him once more. Oh, it was so lovely, I couldn't talk much, the joy was too great. He stroked my cheek and arm a bit awkwardly, played with my curls and our heads lay touching most of the time. I can't tell you, Kitty, the feeling that ran through me all the while. I was too happy for words, and I believe he was as well.

We got up at half-past eight. Peter put on his gym shoes, so that when he toured the house he wouldn't make a noise, and I stood beside him. How it came about so suddenly, I don't know, but before we went downstairs he kissed me, through my hair, half on my left cheek, half on my ear; I tore downstairs without looking round, and am simply longing for to-day!

Yours, Anne

♥

'It's all right,' he assured her, 'don't be frightened.'
And he slipped his arm round her shoulder,
supporting her body against his own. Then he went
on: 'Whatever you do, don't utter a word; just make a
sign, yes or no, or you'll be out of breath again. You
won't mind if I straighten the flowers on your
bodice? The jolt has disarranged them. I'm afraid of
their dropping out, so I'd just like to fasten them a
little more securely.'

She was not used to being made so much fuss of by
men, and she smiled as she answered: 'No, not at all;
I don't mind in the least.'

But he, daunted a little by her answer, and also,
perhaps, to bear out the pretence that he had been
sincere in adopting the stratagem, or even because he
was already beginning to believe that he had been,
exclaimed, 'No, no, you mustn't speak. You'll get
out of breath again. You can easily answer in signs; I
shall understand. Really and truly now, you don't
mind my doing this? Look, there's a little—I think it
must be pollen, spilt over your dress. Do you mind if
I brush it off with my hand? That's not too hard? I'm
not hurting you, am I? Perhaps I'm tickling you a
bit? I don't want to touch the velvet in case I crease
it. But you see, I really had to fasten the flowers; they
would have fallen out if I hadn't. Like that, now; if I
just tuck them a little farther down . . . Seriously, I'm
not annoying you, am I? And if I just sniff them to

see whether they've really got no scent? I don't believe I ever smelt any before. May I? Tell me the truth, now.'

Still smiling, she shrugged her shoulders ever so slightly, as who should say, 'You're quite mad; you know very well that I like it.'

The magic of first love is our ignorance that it can ever end.

Benjamin Disraeli (1804–81)

ARTHUR RUBENSTEIN
MY YOUNG YEARS

'Would you play something for me?' she whispered in a low, soft voice. 'Gladly', I answered, and we went to the piano. Her husband stopped talking and settled himself comfortably on the little sofa, and she pushed one of the armchairs nearer to the piano.

'What will you play?' she asked, putting a vase with dark red roses on the side of the piano stand.

'Something of Chopin,' and I began to play the long D flat Nocturne as though in a trance, inspired by her beauty. The Count closed his eyes; when his chin dropped, a barely audible soft snore announced that he was asleep. When I reached the coda with its pianissimo descending sighs, the Countess, suddenly, leaned forward close to me and, covered by the open stand and the flowers, kissed my mouth with a wild passion. I struck a wrong note, too loudly—the Count woke up, and the charm was broken. We finished our champagne, I kissed her hand several times, with ardor; the Count accompanied me to the door, and I left the house. I never saw either of them again.

♥

There is no greater wonder than the way the face of a young woman fits in a man's mind, and stays there, and he could never tell you why; it just seems it was the thing he wanted.

R.L. Stevenson
Catriona, 1893

When one feels oneself smitten by love for a woman, one should say to oneself, 'Who are the people around her? What kind of life has she led?' All one's future happiness lies in the answer.

Alfred de Vigny
Journal d'un poete, C19

The hardest task of a girl's life is to prove to a man that his intentions are serious.

Helen Rowland
Reflections of a Batchelor Girl, 1903

Amanda: What have you been doing lately? During these last years?

Elyot: Travelling about. I went round the world you know after—

Amanda (hurriedly): Yes, yes, I know. How was it?

Elyot: The world?

Amanda: Yes.

Elyot: Oh, highly enjoyable.

Amanda: China must be very interesting.

Elyot: Very big, China.

Amanda: And Japan—

Elyot: Very small.

Amanda: Did you eat sharks' fins, and take your shoes off, and use chopsticks and everything?

Elyot: Practically everything.

Amanda: And India: the burning Ghars, or Ghats, or whatever they are, and the Taj Mahal. How was the Taj Mahal?

Elyot (looking at her): Unbelievable, a sort of dream.

Amanda: That was the moonlight I expect, you must have seen it in the moonlight.

Elyot (never taking his eyes off her face): Yes, moonlight is cruelly deceptive.

Amanda: And it didn't look like a biscuit box did it? I've always felt that it might.

Elyot (quietly): Darling, darling, I love you so.

Amanda: And I do hope you met a sacred Elephant. They're lint white I believe, and very, very sweet.

Elyot: I've never loved anyone else for an instant.

Amanda (raising her hand feebly in protest): No, no, you mustn't—Elyot—stop.

Elyot: You love me, too, don't you' There's no doubt about it anywhere, is there?

Amanda: No, no doubt anywhere.

Elyot: You're looking very lovely you know, in this damned moonlight. Your skin is clear and cool, and your eyes are shining, and you're growing lovelier and lovelier every second as I look at you. You don't hold any mystery for me, darling, do you mind? There isn't a particle of you that I don't know, remember, and want.

Amanda (softly): I'm glad, my sweet.

Elyot: More than any desire anywhere, deep down in my deepest heart I want you back again—please—

Amanda (putting her hand over his mouth): Don't say any more, you're making me cry so dreadfully.

LOVING ♥ ♥ ♥

And indeed I felt happy with her, so perfectly happy, that the one desire of my mind was that it should differ in nothing from hers, and already I wished for nothing beyond her smile, and to walk with her thus, hand in hand, along a sun-warmed, flower-bordered path.

André Gide
Strait is the Gate, 1948

♥

Love is something far more than desire for sexual intercourse; it is the principal means of escape from the loneliness which affects most men and women throughout the greater part of their lives. Those who have never known the deep intimacy and the intense companionship of mutual love have missed the best thing that life has to give.

Bertrand Russell (1872–1970)

♥

Men are almost heartbreakingly susceptible to love. Much more so than women. A man seldom contracts a mild case. He falls head over heels into raging romance.

Dr. Joyce Brothers
What every woman should know about men, 1982

WILLIAM SHAKESPEARE
SONNET XVIII

Let me not to the marriage of true minds
Admit impediments. Love is not love
Which alters when it alteration finds,
Or bends with the remover to remove:
O, no! It is an ever fixed mark,
That looks on tempests and is never shaken,
It is the star to every wandering bark,
Whose worth's unknown, although his height be
   taken
Love's not Time's fool, though rosy lips and cheeks
Within his bending sickle's compass come;
Love alters not, with his brief hours and weeks,
But bears it out even to the edge of doom.
If this be error and upon me proved,
I never writ, nor no man ever loved.

♥ ♥ ♥

ARNOLD BENNETT TO HIS WIFE

George H. Doran,
25, West 32nd Street,
New York,
23rd November, 1911.

. . . In a fortnight I shall be (I hope) in your arms, and between your breasts. I shall see you and I shall know if you have changed, I mean physically. Otherwise you are not changed, I know it by your letters. The endings of your letters charm me and excite me, horribly. At the bottom of my mind is that every day here bores me, even though I am always amused or interested. Before I saw you I didn't have a moment's real peace. However, by the most extraordinary effort of willpower that I have ever accomplished, I have kept absolutely intact all my vital forces for you. It's killing me. My little one, one understands oneself, I imagine. You will never know exactly how and how much I love you; nobody knows it except me. But you almost know. I kiss you enormously.

Thy A.

6.30

Mitya, it's too awful: I can't sleep, I want you so, I have been lying awake for the best part of an hour, thinking of nothing else. I have opened the window wide, and the fresh, indescribably sweet air soothes my burning cheeks.

I can't wait more than a day or two: we *must* have each other, it is brutal, imperative, and inevitable. Mitya, it is torture: yesterday afternoon was torture, every day that I see you, and can't have you, is torture. I must, I must.

I told you at Monte Carlo it would end like this, in just the bare physical urgency. It *is* ending like this, for me. We are wasting time. We must waste time no longer.

Damn you, Mitya, damn you for your colour, and your beauty, and your health, and your vitality—you make the most irresistible appeal to one's senses that it is possible to make.

I almost hate you for it.

Heavens above! The reason why I'm so jealous of you is obvious enough! If you weren't so damned attractive physically, do you think my heart would beat almost to suffocation whenever I see you speak to someone?

If you don't realise how attractive you are in that way, let me tell you, other people *do*, and have told me so . . .

D.H. LAWRENCE TO FRIEDA WEEKLEY

Waldbröl-Mitwoch [*15th May 1912*]

. . . Can't you feel how certainly I love you and how certainly we shall be married. Only let us wait just a short time, to get strong again. Two shaken, rather sick people together would be a bad start. A little waiting, let us have, because I love you. Or does the waiting make you worse?—no, not when it is only a time of preparation. Do you know, like the old knights, I seem to want a certain time to prepare myself—a sort of vigil with myself. Because it is a great thing for me to marry you, not a quick, passionate coming together. I know in my heart 'here's my marriage'. It feels rather terrible—because it is a great thing in my life—it is *my life*—I am a bit awe-inspired—I want to get used to it. If you think it is fear and indecision, you wrong me. It is *you* who would hurry who are undecided. It's the very strength and inevitability of the oncoming thing that makes me wait, to get in harmony with it. Dear God, I am marrying you, now, don't you see. It's a far greater thing than ever I knew. Give me till next week-end, at least. If you love me, you will understand . . .

♥ ♥ ♥

JAMES JOYCE TO NORA BARNACLE

60 Shelbourne Road
15 August 1904

My dear Nora,

It has just struck me. I came in at half past eleven. Since then I have been sitting in an easy chair like a fool. I could do nothing. I hear nothing but your voice. I am like a fool hearing you call me 'Dear'. I offended two men today by leaving them coolly. I wanted to hear your voice, not theirs.

When I am with you I leave aside my contemptuous, suspicious nature. I wish I felt your head on my shoulder. I think I will go to bed.

I have been a half-hour writing this thing. Will you write something to me? I hope you will. How am I to sign myself? I won't sign anything at all, because I don't know what to sign myself.

♥

ZELDA TO SCOTT FITZGERALD

[*March 1919*]

Sweetheart,

Please, please don't be so depressed—We'll be married soon, and then these lonesome nights will be over forever—and until we are, I am loving, loving every tiny minute of the day and night—Maybe you won't understand this, but sometimes when I miss you most, it's hardest to write—and you always know when I make myself—Just the ache of it all—and I CAN'T tell you. If we were together, you'd feel how strong it is—you're so sweet when you're melancholy. I love your sad tenderness—when I've hurt you—That's one of the reasons I could never be sorry for our quarrels—and they bothered you so—Those dear, dear little fusses, when I always tried so hard to make you kiss and forget—

Scott—there's nothing in all the world I want but you—and your precious love— All the material things are nothing. I'd just hate to live a sordid, colorless existence—because you'd soon love me less—and less—and I'd do anything—anything—to keep your heart for my own—I don't want to live—I want to love first, and live incidentally—Why don't you feel that I'm waiting—I'll come to you, Lover, when you're ready—Don't—don't ever think of the things you can't give me—You've trusted me with the dearest heart of all—and it's so damn much more than anybody else in all the world has ever had—

How can you think deliberately of life without me—If you should die—O Darling—darling Scott—It'd be like going blind. I know I would, too,—I'd have no purpose in life—just a pretty—decoration. Don't you think I was made for you? I feel like you had me ordered—and I was delivered to you—to be worn—I want you to wear me, like a watch—charm or a button hole boquet—to the world. And then, when we're alone, I want to help—to know that you can't do *anything* without me.

♥

True love is like seeing ghosts: we all talk about it but few of us have ever seen one.

La Rochefoucauld (1613–80)

♥

An absence, the decline of a dinner invitation, an unintentional coldness, can accomplish more than all the cosmetics and beautiful dresses in the world.

Marcel Proust (1871–1922)

NAPOLEON TO CITIZENESS JOSEPHINE BONAPARTE

Marmirolo
29 Messidor, Year IV (17 July, 1796)

I have received your letter, my adorable; it has filled my heart with joy. I am grateful for the trouble you have taken to give me your news. Your health should be better today; I feel sure you have recovered. I urge you to go riding; that can't fail to do you good.

. . . I will send your horse; but I hope you will soon be able to join me. A few days ago I thought I loved you; but since I last saw you I feel I love you a thousand times more. All the time I have known you I adore you more each day; that just shows how wrong was La Bruyère's maxim that *love comes all at once.* Everything in Nature has its own life and different stages of growth. I beg you, let me see some of your faults: be less beautiful, less graceful, less kind, less good; but, above all, never be jealous and never cry; your tears drive me mad and burn my blood. Be sure I can't have a thought except of you or an idea I don't tell you about.

Rest thoroughly and get well. Come and join me; before we die let us at least be able to say: 'We had so many happy days!!'

GAVIN EWART
HURRIED LOVE

Those who make hurried love don't do so
from any lack of affection
or because they despise their partner
as a human being—
what they're doing
is just as sincere as a more formal wooing.

She may have a train to catch; perhaps the
room is theirs for one hour only
or a mother is expected back or
some interruption
known, awaited—
so the spur of the moment must be celebrated.

Making love against time is really
the occupation of all lovers
and the clock-hands moving
point a moral:
not crude, but clever
are those who grab what soon is gone for ever.

GUY DE MAUPASSANT
OUR HEARTS

Mariolle's eyes always searched among the letters
for the longed-for handwriting. When he had found
it, an involuntary emotion would surge up in his
heart, making it throb wildly; he always took this
letter first, and would dwell on the address before
tearing open the envelope. What would she say?
Would the word 'love' be there? She had never yet
used that word without adding 'well' or 'very much';
'I love you well' or 'I love you very much'. How
thoroughly he was used to this formula that lost all
power by using additional words! Can there be much
or little in loving?

To love 'very much' is to love poorly: one
loves—that is all—it cannot be modified or
completed without being nullified. It is a short word,
but it contains all: it means the body, the soul, the
life, the entire being. We feel it as we feel the warmth
of the blood, we breathe it as we breathe the air, we
carry it in ourselves as we carry our thoughts.
Nothing more exists for us. It is not a word; it is an
inexpressible state indicated by four letters . . .

♥

GUSTAVE FLAUBERT
MADAME BOVARY

But when she looked at her face in the glass she was surprised by what she saw. Never had her eyes looked so large, so black, so fathomless. Some subtle influence, diffused about her person, had trans-figured her.

She kept on saying to herself: 'I have a lover—a lover!' finding joy in the thought, the joy of girlhood renewed as when she had for the first time realized the claims of her body. So, after all, she was to know the happiness of love! of those fevered moments of delight which she had despaired of finding. She stood on the threshold of a magic land where passion, ecstasy, delirium would reign supreme. A blue immensity was round her: the high peaks of sentiment glittered for her in imagination. Mere ordinary existence seemed a thing far off and tiny, glimpsed far below in the shadows cast by those high immensities.

Then she called to mind the heroines of the books that she had read; the lyrical legion of those adulterous ladies sang in her memory as sisters, enthralling her with the charm of their voices. She became, in her own person, a living part, as it were, of that imaginary world. She was realizing the long dream of her youth, seeing herself as one of those Great Lovers whom she had so much envied. But that was not her only feeling. In what had happened she saw vengeance gratified. She had had more than her share of suffering! Now, at last, she had triumphed, and love, so long repressed, leapt like a living fountain in her heart, bubbling upward in ecstatic freedom. She revelled in it without remorse, without disquiet, without anxiety.

The whole of the next day passed in a sweet delight such as she had never known before. They exchanged vows. She told him of her sorrows . . . Rodolphe silenced her with kisses, and she, looking at him through half-closed eyes, begged him to call her once more by her name, to say again he loved her.

As for being loved, not only does it serve no purpose, it almost always brings disaster. It must be admitted that this is one of the risks you run in loving someone.

Henry de Montherlant
Explicit Mysterium, 1931

WUTHERING HEIGHTS

A movement of Catherine's relieved me a little presently: she put up her hand to clasp his neck, and bring her cheek to his, as he held her: while he, in return, covering her with frantic caresses, said wildly—

'You teach me now how cruel you've been—cruel and false. *Why* did you despise me? *Why* did you betray your own heart, Cathy? I have not one word of comfort—you deserve this. You have killed yourself. Yes, you may kiss me, and cry; and wring out my kisses and tears. They'll blight you—they'll damn you. You loved me—then what *right* had you to leave me? What right—answer me—for the poor fancy you felt for Linton? Because misery, and degradation, and death, and nothing that God or Satan could inflict would have parted us, *you*, of your own will, did it. I have not broken your heart—*you* have broken it—and in breaking it, you have broken mine. So much the worse for me, that I am strong. Do I want to live? What kind of living will it be when you—oh God! would *you* like to live with your soul in the grave?'

'Let me alone. Let me alone,' sobbed Catherine. 'If I've done wrong, I'm dying for it. It is enough! You left me too; but I won't upbraid you! I forgive you. Forgive me!'

THE RAINBOW

'You want me?' she said.

A pallor came over his face.

'Yes,' he said.

Still there was suspense and silence.

'No,' she said, not of herself. 'No, I don't know.'

He felt the tension breaking up in him, his fists slackened, he was unable to move. He stood looking at her, helpless in his vague collapse. For the moment she had become unreal to him. Then he saw her come to him, curiously direct and as if without movement, in a sudden flow. She put her hand to his coat.

'Yes I want to,' she said, impersonally, looking at him with wide, candid, newly-opened eyes, opened now with supreme truth. He went very white as he stood, and did not move, only his eyes were held by hers, and he suffered. She seemed to see him with her newly-opened, wide eyes, almost of a child, and with a strange movement, that was agony to him, she reached slowly forward her dark face and her breast to him, with a slow insinuation of a kiss that made something break in his brain, and it was darkness over him for a few moments.

He had her in his arms, and, obliterated, was kissing her. And it was sheer, blenched agony to him, to break away from himself. She was there so small and light and accepting in his arms, like a child, and yet with such an insinuation of embrace, of infinite embrace, that he could not bear it, he could not stand.

He turned and looked for a chair, and keeping her still in his arms, sat down with her close to him, to his breast. Then, for a few seconds, he went utterly to sleep, asleep and sealed in the darkest sleep, utter, extreme oblivion.

From which he came to gradually, always holding her warm and close upon him, and she as utterly silent as he, involved in the same oblivion, the fecund darkness.

He returned gradually, but newly created, as after a gestation, a new birth, in the womb of darkness. Aerial and light everything was, new as a morning, fresh and newly-begun. Like a dawn the newness and the bliss filled in. And she sat utterly still with him, as if in the same.

Then she looked up at him, the wide, young eyes blazing with light. And he bent down and kissed her on the lips. And the dawn blazed in them, their new life came to pass, it was beyond all conceiving good, it was so good, that it was almost like a passing-away, a trespass. He drew her suddenly closer to him.

CIDER WITH ROSIE

I put down the jar with a gulp and a gasp. Then I turned to look at Rosie. She was yellow and dusty with buttercups and seemed to be purring in the gloom; her hair was rich as a wild bee's nest and her eyes were full of stings. I did not know what to do about her, nor did I know what to do. She looked smooth and precious, a thing of unplumbable mysteries, and perilous as quicksand.

'Rosie . . .' I said, on my knees, and shaking.

She crawled with a rustle of grass towards me, quick and superbly assured. Her hand in mine was like a small wet flame which I could neither hold nor throw away. Then Rosie, with a remorseless, reedy strength, pulled me down from my tottering perch, pulled me down, down into her wide green smile and into the deep subaqueous grass.

Then I remember little, and that little, vaguely. Skin drums beat in my head. Rosie was close-up, salty, an invisible touch, too near to be seen or measured. And it seemed that the wagon under which we lay went floating away like a barge, out over the valley where we rocked unseen, swinging on motionless tides.

Then she took off her boots and stuffed them with flowers. She did the same with mine. Her parched voice crackled like flames in my ears. More fires were started. I drank more cider. Rosie told me outrageous fantasies. She liked me, she said, better than Walt, or Ken, Boney Harris, or even the curate. And I admitted to her, in a loud, rough voice, that she was even prettier than Betty Gleed. For a long time we sat with our mouths very close, breathing the same hot air. We kissed, once only, so dry and shy, it was like two leaves colliding in air.

♥

Time was away and somewhere else,
There were two glasses and two chairs
And two people with the one pulse
(Somebody stopped the moving stairs):
Time was away and somewhere else.

Louis MacNeice (1907–63)
Meeting Point

♥

In love there is always one who kisses and one who offers the cheek.

French Proverb

♥

It is as absurd to say that a man can't love one woman all the time as it is to say that a violinist needs several violins to play the same piece of music.

Honoré de Balzac (1799–1850)

LIVING TOGETHER ♥ ♥ ♥

The particular charm of marriage is the duologue, the permanent conversation between two people who talk over everything and everyone till death breaks the record. It is this back-chat which, in the long run, makes a reciprocal equality more intoxicating than any form of servitude or domination.

Cyril Connolly
The Unquiet Grave, 1944

They that marry where they do not love, will love where they do not marry.

Thomas Fuller
The Holy State and the Profane State, 1642

Love is blind, but marriage restores its sight.

Lichtenberg
Aphorisms 1764–99

Of all actions of a man's life, his marriage does least concern other people; yet of all actions of our life, 'tis the most meddled with by other people.

John Selden
Table Talk, C17

CZAR NICHOLAS II TO THE CZARINA ALEXANDRA
[1915]

My Precious Darling,

My warm and loving thanks for your dear letter, full of tender words, and for both telegrams. I too have you in my thoughts on this our 21st anniversary! I wish you health and all that a deeply loving heart can desire, and thank you on my knees for all your love, affection, friendship and patience, which you have shown me during these long years of our married life!

Today's weather reminds me of that day in Coburg—*how sad it is that we are not together!* Nobody knew that it was the day of our betrothal—it is strange how soon people forget—besides, it means nothing to them . . .

Before the evening I drove along the old road to the town of Slonin in the province of Grodno. It was extraordinarily warm and pleasant; and the smell of the pine forest—one feels enervated and softened!

Always your hubby,
Nicky

I have loved you before for three years (she wrote) with my heart and my mind, but it seems to me I have never loved you *avec mon âme*, as I do now. I love you with all our future life—our life together which seems only now to have taken root and to be alive and growing up in the sun. I do not love you—but Love possesses me utterly: love for you and for our life and for all our richness and joy. I have never felt anything like it before. In fact I did not comprehend the possibility of such a thing. I seem to have only played on the fringe of love, and lived a kind of reflected life that was not really my own, but that came from my past. Now all that is cast away. Oh, my soul, if you come now we shall realize something that it seems to me never has been—such warmth and such richness and such virtue there is in you and me. Is it too late? You are *really* coming?

This morning I went to the little church and prayed. I prayed for us three—for you and me and my brother. It was so gay and yet solemn there.

Come quickly, quickly. My heart will break. Love presses on my forehead like a crown—my head is heavy, heavy. I must not think of you.

♥

JOHN MIDDLETON MURRY ABOUT
KATHERINE MANSFIELD

From the first to the last Katherine appeared to me a totally exquisite being. Everything she did or said had its own manifest validity. I do not think it ever entered my head, at any time, to criticize her in any way. And certainly for a very long while I was secretly astonished that she should have chosen me. Yet life with her was so natural, and so naturally my own, that it seemed that there must be some hidden congruity between our natures; and that idea, which I must needs accept, was at once self-evident and bewildering.

WINSTON TO CLEMENTINE CHURCHILL

You ought to trust me for I do not love and will never love any woman in the world but you, and my chief desire is to link myself to you week by week by bonds which shall ever become more intimate and profound. Beloved I kiss your memory—your sweetness and beauty have cast a glory upon my life. You will find me always

Your loving and
devoted husband W

AN AUTOBIOGRAPHY

I must say I was passionately fond of her. Even at school I used to think of her, and the thought of nightfall and our subsequent meeting was ever haunting me. Separation was unbearable. I used to keep her awake till late in the night with my idle talk. If with this devouring passion there had not been in me a burning attachment to duty, I should either have fallen a prey to disease and premature death, or have sunk into a burdensome existence. But the appointed tasks had to be gone through every morning, and lying to anyone was out of the question. It was this last thing that saved me from many a pitfall.

I have already said that Kasturbai was illiterate. I was very anxious to teach her, but lustful love left me no time. For one thing the teaching had to be done against her will, and that too at night. I dared not meet her in the presence of the elders, much less talk to her. Kathiawad had then, and to a certain extent has even today, its own peculiar, useless and barbarous *Purdah*. Circumstances were thus unfavourable. I must therefore confess that most of my efforts to instruct Kasturbai in our youth were unsuccessful. And when I awoke from the sleep of lust, I had already launched forth into public life, which did not leave me much spare time. I failed likewise to instruct her through private tutors. As a result Kasturbai can now with difficulty write simple letters and understand simple Gujarati. I am sure that, had my love for her been absolutely untainted with lust, she would be a learned lady today; for I could then have conquered her dislike for studies. I know that nothing is impossible for pure love.

♥

ANTON CHEKOV
THE DARLING

Whatever ideas her husband had, she adopted as her own. If he thought that the room was hot or that business was slow, she thought so too. Her husband did not care for entertainments and on holidays stayed home—so did she.

'You are always at home or in the office,' her friends would say. 'You ought to go to the theatre, darling, or to the circus.'

'Vasichka and I have no time for the theatre,' she would answer sedately. 'We are working people, we're not interested in such foolishness. What good are these theatres?'

On Saturdays the two of them would go to evening service, on holidays they attended early Mass, and returning from the church they walked side by side, their faces wearing a softened expression. There was an agreeable aroma about them, and her silk dress rustled pleasantly. At home they had tea with shortbread, and various kinds of jam, and afterwards they ate pie. Every day at noon, in the yard and on the street just outside the gate, there was a delicious smell of *borshch* and roast lamb or duck, and on fast days there was the odour of fish, and one could not pass the Pustovalov gate without one's mouth watering.

In the office the samovar was always boiling and the customers were treated to tea with doughnuts. Once a week the pair went to the baths and returned side by side, both with red faces.

'Yes, everything goes well with us, thank God,' Olenka would say to her friends. 'I wish everyone were as happy as Vasichka and I.'

Marriage may often be a stormy lake, but celibacy is almost always a muddy horse-pond.

Thomas Love Peacock
Melincourt, 1817

It takes patience to appreciate domestic bliss; volatile spirits prefer unhappiness.

George Santayana (1863–1952)

ELIZABETH JENNINGS
ONE FLESH

Lying apart now, each in a separate bed,
He with a book, keeping the light on late,
She like a girl dreaming of childhood,
All men elsewhere—it is as if they wait
Some new event: the book he holds unread,
Her eyes fixed on the shadows overhead.

Tossed up like flotsam from a former passion,
How cool they lie. They hardly ever touch,
Or if they do it is like a confession
Of having little feeling—or too much.
Chastity faces them, a destination
For which their whole lives were a preparation.

Strangely apart, yet strangely together,
Silence between them like a thread to hold
And not wind in. And time itself's a feather
Touching them gently. Do they know they're old,
These two who are my father and my mother
Whose fire from which I came, has now grown cold?

PARTING♥ ♥ ♥

There are very few people who are not ashamed of having been in love when they no longer love each other.

La Rochefoucauld (1613–80)

It is easier to keep half a dozen lovers guessing than to keep one lover after he has stopped guessing.

Helen Rowland
Reflections of a Batchelor Girl, 1903

The heart may think it knows better; the senses know that absence blots people out.

Elizabeth Bowen
The Death of the Heart, 1938

It is very hard to be in love with someone who no longer loves you, but it is far worse to be loved by someone with whom you are no longer in love.

Georges Courteline, 1917

WU-TI EMPEROR OF THE LIANG DYNASTY
(A.D. 464–549)
PEOPLE HIDE THEIR LOVE

Who says that it's by my desire,
This separation, this living so far from you?
My dress still smells of the perfume that you wore;
My hand still holds the letter that you sent.
Round my waist I wear a double sash;
I dream that it binds us both with a same-heart knot.
Did you know that people hide their love,
Like a flower that seems too precious to be picked?

♥

THOMAS HARDY
TESS OF THE D'URBERVILLES

. . . 'Angel, if anything happens to me, will you watch over Liza-Lu for my sake?' she asked, when they had listened a long time to the wind among the pillars.

'I will.'

'She is so good and simple and pure. O Angel—I wish you would marry her if you lose me, as you will do shortly. O, if you would!'

'If I lose you, I lose all! And she is my sister-in-law.'

'That's nothing, dearest. People marry sister-laws continually about Marlott; and 'Liza-Lu is so gentle and sweet, and she is growing so beautiful. O I could share you with her willingly when we are spirits! If you would train her and teach her, Angel, and bring her up for your own self! . . . She has all the best of me without the bad of me; and if she were to become yours it would almost seem as if death had not divided us . . . Well, I have said it. I won't mention it again.'

She ceased, and he fell into thought. In the far north-east sky he could see between the pillars a level streak of light. The uniform concavity of black cloud was lifting bodily like the lid of a pot, letting in at the earth's edge the coming day, against which the towering monoliths and trilithons began to be blackly defined.

'Did they sacrifice to God here?' asked she.

'No,' said he.

'Who to?'

'I believe to the sun. That lofty stone set away by itself is in the direction of the sun, which will presently rise behind it.'

'This reminds me, dear,' she said. 'You remember you never would interfere with any belief of mine before we were married? But I knew your mind all the same, and I thought as you thought—not from any reasons of my own, but because you thought so. Tell me now, Angel, do you think we shall meet again after we are dead? I want to know.'

He kissed her to avoid a reply at such a time.

'O, Angel—I fear that means no!' said she, with a suppressed sob. 'And I wanted to see you again—so much, so much! What—not even you and I, Angel, who love each other so well?'

Like a greater than himself, to the critical question at the critical time he did not answer; and they were again silent . . .

♥

VERA BRITTAIN
TESTAMENT OF YOUTH

But when, suddenly, the shriek of the whistle cut sharply through the tumult of sound, our resolution not to kiss on a crowded platform vanished with our consciousness of the crowd's exasperating presence. Too angry and miserable to be shy any more, we clung together and kissed in forlorn desperation.

'I shan't look out of the window and wave to you,' I told him, and he replied incoherently: 'No—don't; I can't!'

To my amazement, taut and tearless as I was, I saw him hastily mop his eyes with his handkerchief, and in that moment, when it was too late to respond or to show that I understood, I realised how much more he cared for me than I had supposed or he had ever shown. I felt, too, so bitterly sorry for him because he had to fight against his tears while I had no wish to cry at all, and the intolerable longing to comfort him when there was no more time in which to do it made me furious with the frantic pain of impotent desire.

And then, all at once, the whistle sounded again, and the train started. As the noisy group moved away from the door he sprang on to the footboard, clung to my hand and, drawing my face down to his, kissed my lips in a sudden vehemence of despair. And I kissed his, and just managed to whisper 'Good-bye!' The next moment he was walking rapidly down the platform, with his head bent and his face very pale. Although I had said that I would not, I stood by the door as the train left the station and watched him moving through the crowd. But he never turned again . . .

♥

Say what you will, 'tis better to be left than never to have been loved.

William Congreve (1670–1729)

♥

GRAHAM GREENE
THE END OF THE AFFAIR

'Dearest Maurice', she wrote, 'I meant to write to you the other night after you had gone away, but I felt rather sick when I got home and Henry fussed about me. I'm writing instead of telephoning. I can't telephone and hear your voice go queer when I say

I'm not going to come away with you. Because I'm not going to come away with you, Maurice, dearest Maurice. I love you but I can't see you again. I don't know how I'm going to live in this pain and longing and I'm praying to God all the time that he won't be hard on me, that he won't keep me alive. Dear Maurice, I want to have my cake and eat it like everybody else. I went to a priest two days ago . . . and I told him I wanted to be Catholic . . . I said, I'm not really married to Henry any more. We don't sleep together—not since the first year with you . . . I asked him couldn't I be a Catholic and marry you? I knew you wouldn't mind going through a service . . . No, no, no, he said, I couldn't marry you, I couldn't go on seeing you, not if I was going to be a Catholic. I thought to hell with the whole lot of them and I walked out of the room where I was seeing him and I slammed the door to show what I thought of priests. They are between us and God, I thought; God has more mercy . . . only it's such an odd sort of mercy, it sometimes looks like punishment. Maurice, my dearest, I've got a foul headache, and I feel like death. I wish I weren't as strong as a horse. I don't want to live without you, and I know one day I shall meet you on the Common and then I won't care a damn about Henry or God or anything. But what's the good, Maurice? I believe there's a God . . . I've caught belief like a disease. I've fallen into belief like I fell in love. I've never loved before as I love you, and I've never believed in anything before as I believe now . . . I fought belief for longer than I fought love, but I haven't any fight left.

Peter: . . . And I was so happy when we were together—So . . . contented, so . . . at peace: I can't express it; I had never imagined such quiet happiness.
I had only experienced excitement, delirium,
Desire for possession. It was not like that at all.
It was something very strange. There was such . . . tranquillity . . .

Edward: And what interrupted this interesting affair?

(*Enter* Alex *in shirtsleeves and an apron*)

Alex: Edward, I can't find any curry powder.

Edward: There isn't any curry powder. Lavinia hates curry.

Alex: There goes another surprise, then. I must think. I didn't expect to find any mangoes,
But I *did* count upon curry powder.

[*Exit*]

Peter: That is exactly what I want to know.
She has simply faded—into some other picture—
Like a film effect. She doesn't want to see me;
Makes excuses, not very plausible,
And when I do see her, she seems preoccupied
With some secret excitement which I cannot share.

Edward: Do you think she has simply lost interest in you?

Peter: You put it just wrong. I think of it differently.
It is not her interest in *me* that I miss—

But those moments in which we seemed to share
    some perception,
Some feeling, some indefinable experience
In which we were both unaware of ourselves.
In your terms, perhaps, she's lost interest in me.

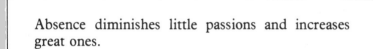

Absence diminishes little passions and increases great ones.

Proverb

Hot love is soon cold.

Proverb

They that too deeply love too deeply hate.

Proverb

Hot love is soon cold.

Proverb

DOROTHY PARKER
A TELEPHONE CALL

Please, God, let him telephone me now. Dear God, let him call me now. I won't ask anything else of You, truly I won't. It isn't very much to ask. It would be so little to You, God, such a little, little thing. Only let him telephone now. Please, God. Please, please, please . . .

. . . I think he must still like me a little. He couldn't have called me 'darling' twice today, if he didn't still like me a little. It isn't all gone, if he still likes me a little; even if it's only a little, little bit. You see, God, if You would just let him telephone me, I wouldn't have to ask You anything more. I would be sweet to him, I would be gay, I would be just the way I used to be, and then he would love me again. And then I would never have to ask You for anything more. Don't You see, God? So won't You please let him telephone me? Won't You please, please, please?

SIMPLE LYRIC

When I think of her sparkling face
And of her body that rocked this way and that,
When I think of her laughter,
Her jubilance that filled me,
It's a wonder I'm not gone mad.

She is away and I cannot do what I want.
Other faces pale when I get close.
She is away and I cannot breathe her in.

The space her leaving has created
I have attempted to fill
With bodies that numbed upon touching,
Among them I expected her opposite,
And found only forgeries.

Her wholeness I know to be a fiction of my making,
Still I cannot dismiss the longing for her;
It is a craving for sensation new flesh
Cannot wholly calm or cancel,
It is perhaps for more than her.

At night above the parks the stars are swarming.
The streets are thick with nostalgia;
I move through senseless routine and insensitive
    chatter
As if her going did not matter.
She is away and I cannot breathe her in.
I am ill simply through wanting her.

FROM DORA CARRINGTON'S DIARY [1932]

February 17th. In the Library

I dreamt of you again last night. And when I woke up it was as if you had died afresh. Every day I find it *harder* to bear. For what point is there in life now? I read all your letters this afternoon. Because I could not bear the utter loneliness here without you. If only I had believed my fears and had never left you for a day. But that would have meant 'encroaching' on your liberty, and breaking the 'laws'. What is the use of anything now without you? I keep on consulting you. But for what purpose? For I can no longer please you. I look at our favourites I try and read them, but without you they give me no pleasure. I only remember the evenings when you read them to me aloud and then I cry. I feel as if we had collected all our wheat into a barn to make bread and beer for the rest of our lives and now our barn has been burnt down and we stand on a cold winter morning looking at the charred ruins. For this little room was the gleanings of our life together. All our happiness was over this fire and with these books. With Voltaire blessing us with up-raised hand on the wall. It was all for you; I loved you so utterly and now there is nothing left to look forward to. You made me so absolutely happy. Every year had grown happier with you. It is impossible to think that I shall never sit with you again and hear your laugh. *That everyday for the rest of my life you will be away*. No one to talk to about my pleasures. No one to call me for walks to go 'to the terrace'. I write in an empty book. I cry in an empty room. And there can never be any comfort again. 'You can't get away from the fact that Lytton is dead', he said.

♥

OSCAR WILDE
THE BALLAD OF READING GAOL

Yet each man kills the thing he loves,
   By each let this be heard,
Some do it with a bitter look,
   Some with a flattering word,
The coward does it with a kiss,
   The brave man with a sword!

Some kill their love when they are young,
   And some when they are old;
Some strangle with the hands of Lust,
   Some with the hands of Gold:
The kindest use a knife, because
   The dead so soon grow cold.

Some love too little, some too long,
   Some sell, and others buy;
Some do the deed with many tears,
   And some without a sigh:
For each man kills the thing he loves,
   Yet each man does not die.

ACKNOWLEDGEMENTS

For permission to reprint copyright material the publishers gratefully acknowledge the following:

P.8, top: *Other People's Letters*, Macmillan Publishers, 1978; p.10; *Anna Karenina*, translated by Rosemary Edmonds, Penguin Books Limited, 1954; p.11: *Bonjour Tristesse*, John Murray Publishers Limited, 1955; p.12: *Anne Frank's Diary*, Vallentine Mitchell & Co. Limited, 1952; pp.14–15: *Swann's Way*, Chatto & Windus, (re-issued); p.16: *My Young Years*, Jonathan Cape Limited, 1973; pp.18–19: *Private Lives*, Eyre Methuen & Company Limited, 1930; p.22, top: *Strait is the Gate*, Martin Secker & Warburg Limited, 1948; p.24: *Arnold Bennett in Love*, David, Bruce & Watson, (O/P); p.25: *A Solitary Woman*, Constable & Co. Limited, 1981; p.26: *Letters of D.H. Lawrence*, Laurence Pollinger Limited, the Estate of Mrs Frieda Lawrence Ravagli and Cambridge University Press, 1979; p.27: *Selected Letters of James Joyce*, Faber and Faber Limited, 1976; pp.28–29: *Zelda Fitzgerald, A Biography*, The Bodley Head Limited, 1970; p.32: *Our Hearts*, Reynall & Hitchcock & Co. Limited, (U.S.A.); pp.33–34: *Madame Bovary*, Oxford University Press, 1981; p.31: *The Collected Ewart 1933–1980*, Hutchinson Books Limited; pp.36–37: *The Rainbow*, Laurence Pollinger Limited, the Estate of Mrs Frieda Lawrence Ravagli and Penguin Books Limited, 1915; pp.38–39: *Cider with Rosie*, The Hogarth Press, 1959; p.39: *The Collected Poems of Louis MacNeice*, Faber and Faber Limited, 1979; pp.44–45 top: *Between Two Worlds*, The Society of Authors and Jonathan Cape Limited, 1935; pp.46–47: *An Autobiography*, The Navajivan Trust and Penguin Books Limited, 1982; pp.47–48: *The Darling*, The Rutledge Press and W. H. Smith, (U.S.A.); p.49: *Collected Poems*, Macmillan Publishers, 1967; p.53: *Chinese Poems*, George Allen & Unwin (Publishers) Limited, 1982; pp.55–56: *Testament of Youth*, Victor Gollancz Ltd., 1933; pp.56–57: *The End of the Affair*, Laurence Pollinger Limited and Heinemann/Bodley Head, 1951; pp.58–59; *The Cocktail Party*, Faber and Faber Limited and Harcourt Brace Jovanovich, Inc., 1950; p.60: *The Collected Dorothy Parker*, Gerald Duckworth & Co. Limited, 1944; p.61: *Love Poems*, George Allen & Unwin (Publishers) Limited, 1981; pp.62–63; *Carrington: Letters and Extracts from her Diaries*, the David Garnett Estate, the Sophie Partridge Trust and Jonathan Cape Limited, 1979.